BUSES
AT WORK

BUSES
AT WORK

STEPHEN MORRIS

LONDON
IAN ALLAN LTD

First published 1982

ISBN 0 7110 1238 5

© Ian Allan Ltd 1982

Published by Ian Allan Ltd, Shepperton, Surrey;
and printed by Ian Allan Printing Ltd at their works
at Coombelands in Runnymede, England

CONTENTS

Front cover: The development of new towns demands new
bus service patterns. Crawley, West Sussex, has a
substantial network of services operated by London Country,
under the C-Line local identity, serving the various housing
areas and industrial estates. Leyland Atlantean AN228
typifies the rolling stock used on C-Line services.
D. Trevor Rowe

Title page: A typical scene in a town in the midst of a rural
area, as passengers board an Alder Valley Plaxton-bodied
Ford bus at Guildford bus station. Since the NBC took a liking
to lightweights for certain applications during the 1970s, the
policy has swung the other way now and most Bedfords and
Fords have been sold off. *J. G. Glover*

Left: The operator licensing regulations of the 1980 Transport
Act require minimum standards of maintenance facilities.
Maintenance for smaller fleets is sometimes contracted out
altogether, but those which opt to do it themselves have a
wide variety of facilities. Possibly the most comprehensive is
London Transport's Aldenham works, where a Routemaster
bus is seen undergoing overhaul. It is highly likely that this
body will be united with a set of running units from another
vehicle altogether and will thus change its identity. *L. J. Long*

INTRODUCTION

To an enthusiast, the fascination of the motorbus concerns the vehicle itself — its history and construction, its sight and sound, and the physical sensation of movement. But to many these finer points are lost: the vehicle and its individual or class characteristics are secondary to its function. *Buses at Work* is an attempt to portray the various functions of the bus — not just as vehicles, but as working vehicles in a working environment; looking at the subject as a method of transport.

The bus is still a major method of transport for many people. It is all too easy to gain the impression that this is the age of the motorcar — the number of cars on our roads is at an all time high level and the media resound to the clamorous advertising campaigns of numerous companies. Nevertheless, the number of people who are reliant on public transport is still surprisingly high. In some areas, London being the classic example, the bus has to vie with the railways as the principal mode of public transport, but in many areas the bus is still most people's way of getting from A to B. Typical journeys for bus users are getting into the centre of a town or city from an outlying suburb or village for work or school or for shopping; and such is the pattern of life that even people from households with access to a car are dependent upon the bus for some of their activities.

The boom period for the bus was the 1950s; postwar affluence had not yet reached the stage where car ownership was the norm, but it had got to a point where people required mobility. It was accepted that the bus was not only a means of getting to work or to the shops, but an important factor in leisure activities. Thus people took buses to the cinema in the evenings (television still being in its infancy), to football on Saturdays, and on Sundays it was useful for getting away from it all to the country.

This leisure function has been reduced considerably now. In some part this is due to the increase in personal motor vehicles, which are more convenient for leisure travel and do not have to conform to service structures or timetabling. However, the main cause for the fall in numbers of bus passengers for this market is the change in leisure activities that has become apparent in the last 20 years — the decline of the cinema and organised sport, the corresponding rise of home entertainments and the increased numbers of people who holiday abroad. Service patterns have had to change as a result of this fall in passengers, with buses becoming increasingly infrequent after the

evening peak — and this trend is bound to continue.

While short-distance travel might have fallen off, the demand for longer-distance services has increased. This is due in part to the effects of the 1980 Transport Act which has encouraged competition in express coaching and, perhaps to a lesser extent, in the excursions and tours market. Bargain fares have lured people back from the train and other forms of transport in droves. Perhaps in years to come this trend will become more widespread and we might see a return to the situation that existed in the 1950s, especially as petrol becomes too scarce a resource for individual use of cars. The first real indication that this might happen came with the 1973 oil crisis. Today, circumstances have stabilised to some extent, but the basic problem still exists and could return at any moment given the fragile political situation in the Middle East and the finite nature of oil as a resource.

However, whatever the future, the bus is still with us and although one tends to think of today's bus as lacking the character and variety of those in days of yore, there is still a surprising amount of variety to delight the eye. People have tried to force the bus into a standard mould but, try as they might, this has proved impossible and still specialised vehicles are required for specialised functions. Despite rationalisation and modernisation, even today many bus routes have so many peculiar quirks that each is almost a specialised function in itself. Rural areas in particular have had to find individual solutions for individual services, and over the last five years or so there has been a noticeable increase in the number of smaller buses, including midibuses and minibuses on the market. In towns, the rear-engine, front entrance double-decker has not always proved to be the answer; again London is the classic example where the traditional format of an engine at the front and entrance at the back has proved more successful. There have also been differing schools of thought on the relative merits of double- and single-deckers and it seems likely that the articulated bus could add a third dimension to this problem.

I have aimed to show something of this variety and to provide some insight, through the medium of photographs, into the way the bus goes about its daily task. The book is divided into sections covering urban buses, rural buses, coaching and contracts (including express, excursions, tours, works and schools' services) with a short section looking behind the scenes to show something of how the bus actually ends up on the road each day and, we hope, stays there.

The urban bus is still part of the life blood of towns and cities. Without it, large sectors of the community would be unable to get in to work, or to maintain the commercial life of the town in greater or lesser ways. A town without buses would quickly grind to a halt, strangled by vast numbers of cars fighting to get into too small an area. The bus in town is still by far the most economical user of road space and also of fuel. In excess of 500 passenger miles per gallon are within its capabilities, whereas even a very economical car fully laden (a rare state) could hope to achieve no more than 200. It is unfortunate that recent legal and political developments have discriminated against buses, denying them some of their potential but still the bus does much through its often mundane daily task to retain some quality of life in our towns and cities.

Rural communities are also surprisingly dependent upon buses. The plight of many villages has been made worse in recent years because pure economic forces often conspire against the rural bus. One pattern to consort this is the emergence of community buses and postbuses. These have proved that if a bus service (in the broader sense) is removed from a community it cannot survive. Britain is still blessed with some very beautiful rural areas, and what better way is there to see them than from one's elevated position in a bus, especially with a relaxed speed allowing one time to take it all in. I hope something of

the beauty of Britain comes over in the rural section of the book.

Up to 1980, coaches had lost much of their appeal as a serious form of inter-city transport, but fare reductions and improvements in the quality of vehicles have once again made the coach a serious contender for this slice of the market. Contract work is probably the least glamorous side of the bus, but is an important source of income for bus operators and again allows people to get to work or school in many parts of the country.

The photographs that follow should speak for themselves in showing that the British bus is still alive and well (if not quite as fit as once it was) and working hard for its place in the community at large. They should also show that variety is not something that died out in the 1960s and there is still much to interest the connoisseur of this fascinating yet workaday means of transport. It just remains for me to express my thanks to the many people whose photographs I have used and to my colleague Simon Forty for his help and support in this compilation.

Stephen C. Morris
Shepperton
February 1982

Below: Passengers wait in Upper Parliament Street in Nottingham to board Trent Leyland National 488 for the lengthy run to Chesterfield. In the background can be seen Nottingham City Transport Leyland Atlanteans on local services. *K. Lane*

URBAN BUSES

The industrial revolution led to an unprecedented growth in the towns of Britain. Hitherto relatively static in both numbers and size, they had served small agricultural communities in the country as historic market towns and local centres of commerce. Following the industrial revolution, some of these commercial centres increased in size to accommodate the marketing function for the new industries, while others — and in some cases new towns altogether — emerged as manufacturing bases. In certain circumstances, this led to single, self-contained

entities: Sheffield, built on the steel industry, was such a town where geographical location limited development. In other areas the nature of the industry was such that a group of towns sprang up within a small area — like the towns based on the south Lancashire cotton industry. Oldham, for example, became the world's largest spinning town. Macclesfield emerged as a town where machinery was built, and also as the centre of a specialised offshoot of textile production — the manufacture of silk. Manchester became the commercial centre and, after the building of the ship canal, was able to carry out the importing and exporting function.

Once industry had developed there was a need for mass passenger transport. This was provided initially by horsebus services which sprang up in the 1820s and 1830s and were then superseded by tramways. After World War 1 the motorbus began to oust the tram and ultimately proved a more flexible and economical alternative. Although most bus services began as a result of private enterprise, most towns had municipal transport systems by the beginning of the Great War. In some towns, however, services were supplied by company operators, the most notable being Bristol and Oxford. In the former case, a joint transport committee was formed in 1937, but in practice, although the agreement still holds day-to-day, operation is by the Bristol Omnibus Co Ltd. In other towns, most notably in Yorkshire, the railway companies were also involved in bus operation, again through the medium of joint transport committees. Sheffield, Huddersfield, Halifax and Todmorden all had joint committee operations.

The biggest upheaval came in the 1970s when the municipal operators of certain large conurbations were combined into passenger transport executives. The first four, based on the Manchester, Liverpool, Newcastle and Birmingham areas, were formed towards the end of 1969, a fifth emerged in Glasgow in 1972 and more followed the 1974 local government reorganisation in West and South Yorkshire. These brought about integration of bus services in the areas concerned to allow a more structured approach to transport planning.

London is more of a law unto itself. As is well known, the pattern of various independent operators was slowly replaced with the formation in 1933 of the London Passenger Transport Board, which exists today in a modified form. This is a much-simplified description of the position in London, and various works exist which chronicle the history of London Transport in depth.

Surprisingly, a number of independent operators still penetrate some urban areas; most work in from outside but some, such as Mayne's of Manchester, still manage to exist totally within the area of a major transport operator.

A typical urban scene in the centre of Birmingham. YOX 210K was one of 200 Park Royal-bodied Daimler Fleetline CRG6s taken into the West Midlands fleet during 1971/2. 4210 is seen at Stephenson Place. *T. W. Moore*

Above: On a suburban local service in Dumbartonshire is this Central SMT Alexander-bodied Leyland Leopard. The loading is typical of such a service out of the peak hours, and whilst the 36ft Leopard is possibly a bit unwieldy for that type of operation it is not always economical to have smaller vehicles available for such workings. T154's lady driver manages a smile for the camera! *John McIntyre*

Below: Although a few operators managed to operate such vehicles with just one man, this was a compromise solution and the economic necessity to move to one-man operation led to the early demise of the forward-entrance, half-cab double-decker. In 1966 Eastern Scottish obtained 25 new extra-long specimens of the Bristol Lodekka FLF6G. Here Dalkeith-based late survivor, AA213, is seen at North Bridge, Edinburgh on the frequent group of services to Gorebridge in the summer of 1981. *A. Moyes*

Above: Not all it might seem! With the destination shown as Mull via Iona, this Eastern Scottish Leyland National 2 would appear to be on a tour of the Scottish islands rather than a journey round mundane estates in Airdrie. *Iain MacGregor*

Below: Numbered MRO1 this was the first Leyland Olympian for the Scottish Bus Group. It was exhibited at the Motor Show in 1980 and then joined the Alexander (Midland) fleet. It was photographed on 20 February 1981 when it was undergoing comparison trials with a Metrobus, a Fleetline and an Ailsa on typical suburban/urban services on the outskirts of Glasgow, hence the large TB4 number.
OMS 910W later went to work in Aberdeen with Alexander (**Northern**). *John Burnett*

Left: It is often in conditions such as these that buses come into their own, being expected to carry on when motorists decide to leave the car at home. Lothian Region Leyland Atlantean GFS 449N is seen Leith during a snow storm in January 1981. *John Allison*

Left: Several operators have found smaller buses useful on certain specific applications. Whilst they have sometimes proved an invaluable solution to rural transport problems, they have their uses in certain urban/suburban situations. This Ford/Alexander was new to Grampian in 1976 and as that operator's 83 is seen in the Seaton district of Aberdeen later the same year. *Edward Shirras*

Left: The PDR series Atlantean is now extinct in the Strathclyde PTE fleet, and LA578 was one of the last survivors. As will be seen from the notice below the windscreen, Strathclyde has opted for a no-change system. This has benefits in that the driver never handles cash; as the passenger drops his money into a sealed vault it has much reduced the incidence of attacks on drivers, and it also reduced waiting times at stops. But it is often seen by the passenger as a reduction in the level of service . . . *Iain MacGregor*

Left: Town operation is by no means the sole preserve of large public undertakings. This is one of two Glasgow-style Leyland AN68A/1R Alexander-bodied buses with Graham Bus Service Ltd of Paisley, one of several independent operators giving urban services in central Scotland. L10 is seen in Paisley. *T. E. Sutch*

Left: Another independent operator in the Paisley area is Paton Bros Ltd, Renfrew. It operates this Duple-bodied Leopard, SSU 397R, which has bus seating in a coach shell. Here, it arrives in Paisley from Renfrew Ferry in 1979. This type of vehicle is something of a rarity but combines a certain stylishness with practicality. *M. Fowler*

Left: A vehicle such as this East Lancs-bodied Dennis Dominator is often the preserve of larger operators. However, this one was bought new by A1 Service, Ardrossan, for local town services. Dennis is better placed than some manufacturers to supply small quanitites to customers. ECS 58V is seen in Glasgow Street, Ardrossan. *T. E. Sutch*

Above left: Northern General 4677 is a Leyland National 2. Although a typical standard NBC bus it is in the smart dark blue/white livery once worn by the Sunderland District subsidiary. It is seen here setting off from Newcastle.
John Burnett

Below left: The Passenger Transport Executives were established to achieve coordination of services in large urban areas. In Tyne & Wear this has extended to the repainting of some NBC buses in either full T&WPTE colours or an approximation thereof. United 817 is based at Gallowgate depot in the heart of Newcastle, and is one of five Bristol VRTs with 70-seat ECW bodywork featuring coach seats. These were United's first vehicles painted to form part of corporate image on routes serving the Tyne & Wear area.
G. Coxon

Above: A familiar and busy city-centre bus terminus is that at Worswick Street, Newcastle, where the longer-distance Northern General routes begin. Nine vehicles are to be seen in this view in August 1980. Although by that time the Routemaster (far right) had but a few months to go, it was still used in the trunk route to Durham. The Routemasters were usually to be found on long runs and amassed considerable mileages in their 15-year lifespans.
Adrian Pearson

Below: Unlike many municipals, Darlington has opted for 100% single-deck working, using Autofare no-change fare collection. 74 is a Marshall-bodied Dennis Dominator, while 83 is a Marshall-bodied Daimler Fleetline which was acquired from Tyne & Wear. Strangely, both vehicles are on chassis designed for double-deckers! *M. Fowler*

Above: Like Central Scotland, north-east England abounds with independent operators on services which would often seem to be more likely territory for a public undertaking. This Trimdon Motor Service Duple bus-bodied Leyland Leopard takes on a good load in Stockton High Street on No 69 service to Bishop Auckland in September 1981. *Kevin Lane*

Below: Inevitably some independent operators working in pte territory are ripe for takeover, and Economic, Whitburn, has been absorbed into Tyne & Wear PTE. Prior to that event, Economic's 18, a Bedford YRQ with Willowbrook B47F bodywork, was seen at Seaburn on its way from South Shields to Sunderland on Saturday 22 March 1972, when a full standing load was being carried. *I. S. Carr*

Above: The lot of buses has been improved by priority schemes in certain towns. In the pedestrianisation of Manchester's two main thoroughfares, Market Street and Deansgate, buses were still given access, although this was reduced in time. A procession of Greater Manchester Transport buses heads out of Piccadilly into Market Street. *W. M. Ewing*

Below: Merseyside PTE is unique amongst PTEs in that it operates ferries as well as land-bound transport. Bus/ferry coordination on Merseyside is seen here at Birkenhead, with Merseyside Atlanteans and a Crosville dual-purpose Leyland National at Birkenhead Ferry. The skyline is dominated by Liverpool's gargantuan Anglican cathedral on the opposite bank of the Mersey. *A. R. J. Frost*

Above: This was a typical Stockport scene before the new bus station rid Mersey Square of its bus stops. Those in the background of this photograph ceased to be used when the first phase of development opened, and the travel facilities were demolished. The new station lies to the right of the A6 road bridge along which a former Manchester Mancunian Daimler Fleetline is passing towards Manchester. The Greater Manchester area is a classic example of a conurbation with several medium-sized towns surrounding the large city, or in this case pair of cities, in the middle. Traditionally it was ideal bus territory, but passenger numbers have still declined. Two generations of Leyland Titan are evident in this view, with a modern TN15 on route 365 and two of Stockport's trusty PDs. *M. S. Stokes*

Below: Greater Manchester 4006, a Leyland Titan TN15, is photographed in Oldham, on a typical Manchester area trunk route. It had started out in a Pennine village and was working through one of the satellite towns, Oldham, to central Manchester. *J. L. Manley*

Top: GMT 7341, one of a large batch of Northern Counties-bodied Daimler Fleetlines, seen on the 579 to Morris Green, amid modern housing developments on the outskirts of Bolton. *John Robinson*

Above: Although Alderley Edge is outside Greater Manchester County, it is served by GMT buses as well as Crosville, on services inherited from North Western. Usually the E29 was a Crosville service to Macclesfield from Manchester, but GMT had occasional short workings to Alderley. Awaiting the time for its return to Manchester is GMT Leyland National 183 seen here during a layover at Alderley Bank. It would return as a 152X, a GMT service. Since this photograph the E29 has become the 129 and is joint with GMT right through to Macclesfield. *R. Bracegirdle*

Above left: Such is the volume of vehicular traffic these days, that bus priority schemes in urban areas are vital to efficient transport. Britain has been lamentably slow in introducing such schemes, but one of the most adventurous is the Runcorn Busway, where buses enjoy 10½ miles of specially-built reserved road. A Crosville Bristol RELL6G, SRG 140, exchanges passengers at the Busway stop at Shopping City in Runcorn New Town. The Runcorn Busway logotype is evident on the stop flag. *John Mills*

Below left: Another view of the Runcorn Busway at Shopping City in May 1981 with a collection of Crosville vehicles. *Adrian Pearson*

Chester is an example of a small provincial city. It has quite a wide hinterland and its resident population is swelled by tourists. It has a municipal undertaking with a range of interesting vehicles and is the home of Crosville, which looks after the longer-distance services. Above: This CCT Dennis Dominator is seen in Chester in September 1981, whilst Crosville Bristol VR DVG546 is seen (below) on route C53, a local service, at about the same time. DVG546 is one of the buses bought by Crosville from Southdown in 1981. *Both: Adrian Pearson*

Above left: Warrington had a batch of Leyland Titan PD2/40 Specials in 1965. Their specification was somewhat archaic, in that not only were they vacuum-braked but they were built to a width of 7ft 6in. They survived for 15 years or more and No 47 is seen here in a busy town centre towards the end of its days. Had it been capable of omo it could doubtless have worked happily for at least five years more; the PD2 (and PD3) was quite indestructable. *D. R. Wootton*

Below left: Bus operation in seaside resorts is generally on the quiet side in the winter; come summer and passengers are almost fighting to board as shown by this Ribble Leyland Atlantean AN68 with 73-seat Park Royal bodywork, No 1359, in Morecambe. *G. Coxon*

Above: Somehow or other independent operator A. Mayne has managed to retain its Droylsden-Manchester service, even though it works in the heart of Greater Manchester Transport territory. Service 213 is theoretically joint between GMT and Mayne, but in practice Mayne operates all the journeys. Although the concern's AEC Regents are no more, its Roe-bodied Fleetlines and Bristol VRTs in the smart red livery give welcome relief to the virtually solid diet of orange now experienced in Manchester. GMT Metrobus 5101 is thwarted in its attempt to wait on its stand for service 98 in Stevenson Square by a parked lorry, whilst Mayne Fleetline LRJ 213P, working in from Droylsden, has to swing wide to get past to its own stop in the square. *M. Fowler*

Below: An 11.3m Leyland National in service with John Fishwick & Sons Ltd, Leyland. Fishwick is another north-western bus-operating independent which is still thriving, and it has retained its distinguished, if sombre, two shades of green livery. With its proximity to Leyland Vehicles is operates some strange vehicles, including a prototype Titan and a unique AN69 Atlantean. There are not many English independent operators with Leyland Nationals bought new. *Leyland Vehicles*

Above: One of the most go-ahead urban operators is South Yorkshire PTE which has adopted certain European ideas, such as a highly-subsidised service. Another European idea is the articulated bus, which, as is well known, was tried experimentally by SYPTE on the Sheffield City Clipper for about two years. During this period MAN 2004 is seen passing Roe-bodied Leyland-DAB 2010 in Sheffield city centre. *T. W. Moore*

Below: Once a typical Sheffield scene — Leyland-DAB articulated bus 2010 passes Metrobus 454 by Midland station in March 1981. *A. R. Kaye*

Above: Although Barnsley is in the SYPTE area, most of its services are operated by Yorkshire Traction. Barnsley bus station on a September Saturday in 1980 with a representative selection of the YTC fleet. *M. S. Stokes*

Below: South Yorkshire experienced vehicle shortages in 1981/2, resulting in the hire of vehicles from various operators in the north. Out of its home town of Kingston-upon-Hull, this Atlantean is working in Sheffield on hire to South Yorkshire in April 1981, and a busy scene of resident buses. *T. W. Moore*

Above: Some towns are increasingly aware of the need for bus/rail coordination and have accordingly built bus/rail interchanges. This is the transport interchange at Bradford, one of the better examples as seen on 19 March 1977. The occasion was the opening of the interchange, hence the presence of such exotic vehicles as a 1940 Leeds AEC Regent and a 1948 Manchester Crossley, the roofs of which are visible behind the nearest shelter. *David Bailey*

Left: A gaggle of South Yorkshire buses on a dual-carriageway in Doncaster. 426, an Ailsa with distinctive Van Hool bodywork, leads the way with a similar vehicle behind and an Atlantean thundering up the outside. Whilst such roads can speed journey times they often increase mileage without rendering extra passengers. In some less enlightened centres, bypasses take buses away from centres of attraction, where a very short section of bus-only road might have caused considerable improvement to the bus service. *I. P. Cowley*

Above: Several cities make use of NBC services rather than providing a municipal service. In York, West Yorkshire provides local services. Traditionally, the fleetname 'York-West Yorkshire' was used for such services which are controlled by the local authority. In recent years this has given way to the fleetname 'York' with both NBC logos and York City crests. Bound for Chapelfields on route 8 is this York Bristol VRT No 3767. *Adrian Pearson*

Below: The opulence of the Dock Office in Victoria Square, Hull, dominates this Metro-Scania Metropolitan of Kingston-upon-Hull Corporation Transport, No 416 of 1975. *T. W. Moore*

Right: One-man operation in Northampton. The double-decker is an Alexander-bodied Bristol VRTSL, powered by a Gardner engine, while the single-decker is a Willowbrook-bodied Fleetline. Behind the Fleetline is one of the Roe-bodied Daimler CVG6s, a few of which were still operational in 1982. Northampton is another example of a typical medium-sized provincial town with the corporation providing local services and NBC subsidiary United Counties working in from further afield. *T. W. Moore*

Below: Large-scale one-man operation has often led to the fitting of elaborate fare collection equipment to speed journey times. Several operators have adopted the Autofare no-change system. The latest version is the electronic Autofare 3 system, seen here in use on a Nottingham Atlantean, **No 448.** *Control Systems Ltd*

Right: The Dennis Dominator has become a useful tool in many municipal fleets, and even one pte has standardised on it. Most operators have found availability and fuel consumption figures to be most impressive. The first of Leicester's Dennis Dominators entered service early in November 1977. No 233 is pictured here on 15 November in Humberstone Gate. Leicester was the first operator of the type and has now standardised upon it. *T. W. Moore*

Below: Like Paton Bros, Renfrew, shown earlier, Nottingham had several Duple Dominant coach bodies with bus seats. A Leyland Leopard with Duple 'E' bodywork is seen in Queen Street in March 1979. This is one of the 35 examples purchased by the City of Nottingham — something of an unusual sight in service with a large municipal. *T. W. Moore*

Above left: A Northampton VRT bodied by Alexander is pursued out of the town centre by ECW-bodied example in the United Counties fleet in January 1981. *Kevin Lane*

Below left: A City of Nottingham Daimler Fleetline CRG6LX with Northern Counties H47/30D bodywork at University Boulevard on 15 April 1980 en route from Beeston to the city centre. By far for the largest part of urban operation is made up of services from outyling areas into the city or town centre. *G. B. Wise*

Above: In addition to arterial routes, most towns and cities have peripheral routes as well. Leicester City Transport's Dennis Falcon No 90 had a brief spell in service on the route of the same number, the Outer Circle, during April 1981 before returning to Dennis for promotion work. Here No 90 is seen at Victoria Park Road. *M. W. Greenwood*

Below: Oxford is another centre like York where local services are supplied by an NBC company. City of Oxford Motor Services provides a very comprehensive local service for the city, mainly without revenue support, together with a wider network of services from outlying towns. One of its principal trunk routes is that to Aylesbury. A City of Oxford dual-door VRT, No 503, climbs up into Aylesbury with a working from Oxford in August 1981. *Kevin Lane*

Left: Chesterfield Transport's No 55 is a Leyland Panther which was acquired from Merseyside PTE. It is seen here on only its second day in service for Chesterfield, 2 July 1977. It seemed at one time as if rear-engined single-deckers would take over most urban bus services at one time, and a good many undertakings invested quite heavily in the type. With the notable exception of the Bristol RE, most proved unreliable and the double-decker provided a more civilised means of transport with a higher proportion of seated passengers. Liverpool Corporation took large numbers of Panthers, but all had been withdrawn by its successor Merseyside PTE by 1982. Quite a number saw further service in Chesterfield. *M. Fowler*

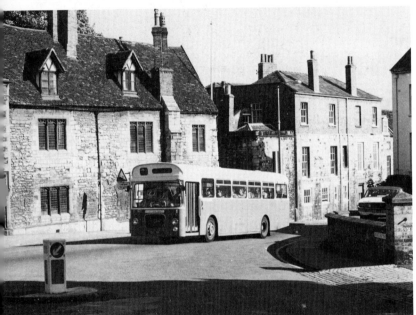

Left: Lincoln too went for the Panther during the 1960s. One of Lincoln's earlier Leyland Panthers, No 46 of the 1968 batch, is seen here climbing Minster Yard, near the Cathedral, on 27 September 1978, one route 8. All of Lincoln's Panthers too are now withdrawn. Lincoln's vehicles have quite a tough time on services past the old part of the city, and they have a considerable pull up the hill to the Cathedral and castle. *G. B. Wise*

Left: One area in which the bus could become a useful tool of traffic management is in the Park and Ride concept, whereby motorists leave their cars at car parks well out of the city and complete their journeys on cheap and efficient services. This ex-London Transport DMS is now operated by Oxford/South Midland on such a service which has so far been a great success. This photograph at Gloucester Green bus station shows the vehicle in its special livery. Alongside is a Duple Dominant IV-bodied Leyland Leopard on the same operator's frequent London service, which has also proved to be a great success, thanks mainly to the marketing effort put into it in recent years. Other operators would do well to note the value of effective marketing . . . *John Marsh*

Above: Birmingham City Transport dabbled in the rear-engine single-deck fashion of the 1960s. Its AEC Swifts did not last long but these strange-looking single-deck Fleetlines, looking like cut-down double-deckers, were much more successful. In the late 1970s and early 1980s the Marshall-bodied Daimler Fleetlines of 1965 could be seen working the Birmingham 'Centrebus' services having replaced newer Commer 19-seaters. This is the type of specialised service for which various types of single-deckers are well-suited, from the load it is engorging, the 19-seat Commers were clearly inadequate for the job. *T. W. Moore*

Below: After cessation of Fleetline production, West Midlands PTE has standardised on the Metrobus. This new example was seen on route 50 to Maypole in September 1981. In this form, the Metrobus in an integral double-decker and until the Leyland Titan reappears on the open market is the only such vehicle readily available to operators. *Adrian Pearson*

Above: A number of operators experimented with Dial-a-Bus services as an alternative mode of transport in suburban areas. This West Midlands Dial-a-Bus service is seen in the Knowle area operated by a Ford A/Alexander integral midibus. *Mark Alexander*

Below: Like Greater Manchester, the West Midlands area comprises a large centre, with its own suburbs and several satellite towns with their own suburbs. Originally Coventry was outside the scope of West Midlands PTE but local government reorganisation of 1974 brought that city into the West Midlands County. Consequently this former Coventry Daimler Fleetline was operated by West Midlands and by 1976 was based at the former Midland Red Hartshill garage, a good way from its former home. It is seen here in another satellite town, Dudley. It could, and no doubt often has, been argued that it was stretching a point to include Coventry as part of West Midlands County as it is large enough in its own right to be an epicentre, and is some miles distant from the epicentre of West Midlands, ie Birmingham. *A. Moyes*

Top: This East Lancs-bodied Fleetline was originally ordered by Coventry Transport, but entered service with West Midlands. It was used to replace much older Birmingham City Transport buses on the Outer Circle service. Here 6731 is seen at Acocks Green in June 1977, on typical Outer Circle territory. Note that at that time the characteristic BCT bus stop was still in place, as was the check clock where conductors would have had to stamp a time card to show that they had not passed before time. *T. W. Moore*

Above: Another well-scattered Coventry bus, again in typical suburban territory. This time seen working from Wolverhampton on route 63 in 1976 is No 4446, a Bristol RE formerly operated by Coventry. *T. W. Moore*

Above: The Stoke-on-Trent area is a conglomeration of five towns, plus smaller communities between. As it is not served by municipal operators it had no need of a pte, the bulk of services being provided by NBC operator Potteries Motor Traction. PMT became the host of an experimental Foden NC and a Dennis Dominator and despite the ceasing of Foden bus production, the NBC operational testing model double-decker remains in operation at Newcastle. It was photographed in service at Audley in April 1981. *A. Moyes*

Below: Stafford local services are now provided by Midland Red (North) since the breakdown of Midland Red into smaller operating units. Midland Red was the instigator of the now universal MAP (market analysis project), which, for better or worse, has recast NBC and other services throughout the country. That for the Stafford/Cannock area is known as Chaserider, after the local Cannock Chase. Here, a Midland Red Chaserider Leyland National is seen in Stafford on a suburban service to Baswich. *M. Fowler*

Left: In addition to PMT, and to a lesser extent Trent and Midland Red, the Stoke area is well covered by independents; one of these is Stonier, Goldenhill. One of Stonier's two ex-Maidstone Northern Counties-bodied Leyland Atlanteans, is seen climbing away into Hanley from Bentille in August 1977. *A. Moyes*

Below: As Midland Red has withdrawn many services, there has been some growth of independents in Staffordshire. Stevensons of Uttoxeter has expanded the scope of its operations in recent years and operates several ex-London Transport DMSs. This example is seen on its two-hourly service to Stafford. This was the first DMS to enter service in the latest livery with a black and white stripe sweeping upwards between the decks towards the rear. Behind is an unusual Leyland Olympian of the first kind, which was a lightweight version of the MCW-Leyland Olympic, with Tiger Cub-type running units, in the fleet of Warstone (Green Bus Service), Great Wyrley. Warstone is now well-known for its immaculate fleet of interesting vehicles. *J. Hall-Lane*

Above: A Willowbrook-bodied Daimler Fleetline heads a line of Cardiff Fleetlines in Castle Street on a busy Saturday morning. The second Fleetline in the row, No 490 with Park Royal bodywork, is working the Llanrumney service, one of those which CK Coaches ran in competition following the ending of CCT's monopoly. *J. Callow*

Below: With Swansea docks and a refinery for a backdrop, a South Wales Leyland National climbs up the 1 in 5.6 gradient of Pen y graig Road en route to the Townhill area of Swansea. 741 is one of the number of Nationals with all-over advertisements for Buckleys Beers, hence the 'Cheer up, Here's the Bus' sticker. *S. K. Miles*

Above: In the midst of a council estate, one of Cardiff's Willowbrook-bodied Bristol VRTs, No 302, picks up passengers for town. As is the case with many off-peak journeys a good proportion of the passengers are pensioners. *M. S. Curtis*

Below: The Metro-Scania vied with the Leyland National as the first of the second-generation rear-engined saloons. It enjoyed a modest popularity, but is not so common now. Two South Welsh municipals, Newport and Taff Ely, still operate a quantity. Here, Taff Ely Metro-Scania No 15 leaves Pontypridd via the low railway bridge at the station. This is an obvious case where single-deckers are necessitated by physical constraints, although Taff Ely uses mainly single-deck vehicles in any case. Shadowed fleet-numbers look a little odd on this type of vehicle. *Ian N. Lynas*

Above: Although the halfcab is now quite a rarity, two NBC subsidiaries, Bristol and Eastern Counties, have retained Bristol Lodekkas for front-line urban service. Bristol Omnibus No 7166 is a FLF6B built in 1964 and seen in Bristol during September 1981. Many crew-operated services in Bristol are still operated by such vehicles; one-man operation is not always appropriate on such workings. *Michael H. C. Baker*

Below: Double-deck omo services in Bristol are mainly in the hands of dual-door Bristol VRTs. Bristol No C5101 on a route 23 (Lockleaze-Centre-Shirehampton), leaves the city centre for College Green. *Viewfinder*

Above: In an attractive setting, which would doubtless be described by estate agents as a mature residential area, is Bristol's Leyland National No C1411 at Clifton on route 83, Broadmead-Clifton-Cheltenham Road. When this photograph was taken, Cheltenham-based C1411 still carried the traditional Bristol fleetname. Like the unusual fleetnames used on York-West Yorkshire vehicles this was a concession to the municipal involvements of the company. *Viewfinder*

Below: Lodekkas also had extended lives at Swindon. This FLF of Bristol was working a service linking new housing at Highworth with Swindon in May 1981. *B. A. Wright*

Left: Smaller market towns often have a similar pattern of service to larger cities, albeit on a smaller scale, although in recent years offpeak services have been thinned considerably. Western National 1100, a very standard NBC ECW-bodied Bristol VRT, amasses a reasonable load on a Taunton local service. *Viewfinder*

Below left: An aerial view of the Royal Parade, Plymouth showing 11 Plymouth City Transport buses, six Leyland National and five Atlanteans. *M. S. Curtis*

Right: Eastern Counties Lodekkas were still operating on local Cambridge routes in December 1980. FLF465 was on the cross-city route 185. Apart from those which went to Scotland in exchange for VRTs in the early 1970s and the sale of some acquired secondhand Eastern Counties' fleet of Bristol FLFs was intact at the beginning of 1982, despite the fact that most of its early VRTs had gone. *Kevin Lane*

Right: An Eastern Counties Leyland National 2, LN612, on a local Cambridge service in December 1980. The uninitiated can do no more than guess at its destination, the display 'Service' having been popular with certain ex-Tilling concerns for rather too many years. *Kevin Lane*

Right: In mid-November 1980 Norwich County Council commenced an experimental bus service linking car parks and shopping areas under the title 'Shopper Hopper', using Alexander-bodied Leyland Leopards hired from Eastern Counties. Norwich is yet another example of a major town reliant upon NBC for its buses. *R. A. Flower*

Above: Ipswich too started a 'Shopper Hopper' service, for Christmas 1980 and this was worked by its AEC Regent Vs. *I. P. Cowley*

Left: Before its spell on the Shopper Hopper service is Ipswich Borough Transport No 60 on route 3 working in Spring Road on 19 July 1980, the last day of regular crew operated services in Ipswich. However, the Regents were still kept for peakhour work etc. Ipswich seems to have a good collection of daredevil graffiti artists, judging by the viaduct parapet. One hopes that Helen was suitably touched by her elevated birthday ode! *I. P. Cowley*

Above right: Eastern National Bristol RELL6G No 1529 climbs Dovercourt High Street on a route 103 Harwich/ Colchester working in 1980. *A. R. J. Frost*

Below right: Eastern Counties VR188 approaches Felixstowe Ferry on a local town service through rather bleak terrain one sunny evening in May 1977. The scenery clearly did little to attract passengers that evening. *A. R. J. Frost*

Above: Reading Transport 267, a Bristol RE, is seen here in Reading High Street on route 10, sporting that wellknown Reading destination 'Stations'. *Adrian Pearson*

Below: Mole Valley uses this Ford Transit on its lightly-used route 7 between Esher and Surbiton which partially replaced London Transport's 201. Photographed at Surbiton in late December 1981. *John Marsh*

Above: Despite the new bus station at Staines, London Transport route 218 still uses the long-closed Staines West station as its terminus. LS273 is still a regular 218 performer, but it no longer rubs shoulders with Golden Miller service 606 at this point, Golden Miller preferring the delights of the bus station. Golden Miller of Feltham purchased this Leyland Leopard from Ribble; it dates from 1965 and has Marshall bodywork. The company has a network of four routes, all in the western extremity of London Transport. *L. D. S. Dolan*

Below: Seen in Tring while on a Aylesbury-Luton journey in August 1981 is United Counties VRT No 910 carrying an all over advertisement for National Holidays, of a style to be seen in most NBC fleets; it also has coach-type seats. Aylesbury is quite a crossroads for NBC fleets with services of United Counties, City of Oxford, Alder Valley and London Country all working in from surrounding towns. *Kevin Lane*

Left: Much of London Country's operating territory is in the most car-orientated area of England. Typical of such places is Walton-on-Thames where RP32, once a Green Line coach but now demoted to bus work, is seen on the St Peter's Hospital service via Weybridge and Addlestone. Since this view, the 461 has been extended beyond St Peter's Hospital via Chertsey and Shepperton to Feltham in a large loop.
L. D. S. Dolan

Centre left: The shape of things to come? So this line up at Stevenage bus station might have seemed at the time in March 1973. The three types shown were employed on SuperBus local semi-express services. From left to right, they are London Country AEC Swift SM498, Leyland National LN3 and Metro-Scania MS3. This was quite a bold experiment at the time, and the buses were painted in a smart yellow and blue livery with huge SB logos on the sides. In those days it seemed that such vehicles would take over from the previous usual methods; it was not to be despite the favour such buses find abroad.
G. R. Mills

Bottom left: Unlike other NBC subsidiaries London Country has standarised on the Leyland Atlantean for double-deckers. AN259 is seen here at Crawley bus station, on the trunk 455 to Croydon. Crawley has become the centre for an impressive network of local services, serving relatively new housing developments and industrial estates.
Michael Dryhurst

Above right: To cope with its car-orientated operating area London Country has aimed at improving its image. Part of this improvement has been effected by the use of smart coaches on Green Line routes. A Green Line RS (AEC Reliance/Plaxton Supreme) loads in Tring while working the London-bound 708 from Aylesbury in August 1981.   *Kevin Lane*

Below right: Despite the influx of new coaches in recent years, Leyland Nationals with bus seats often end up duplicating Green Line services, rather tarnishing their image. Looking slightly the worse for wear is the B-series National, SNB497, at Luton bus station on 18 December 1980 while working the southbound 717.   *Kevin Lane*

Left: The most intensive urban operation in the UK is understandably in London. It seems that more modern types have had difficulty coping with the conditions — according to London Transport at least. Here, Routemasters battle with heavy traffic in Fleet Street on 25 June 1980. *I. P. Cowley*

Below: For a time London Transport ran a Shoplinker service between Oxford Street and Knightsbridge, the two most popular shopping areas of the capital. It ran at a flat fare of 30p, using Routemasters in a special red and yellow livery. It did not prove a success. Two RMs, 2172 and 2154, are seen here at Hyde Park while working the now-defunct service. *IAL*

Right: The group of services where standard single-deckers have proved most successful in Central London are the Red Arrows. Surprisingly, the ill-fated AEC Merlins worked out their last days on these intensive routes, despite having been unable to cope with less arduous routes elsewhere. Two MBA class Merlins are seen here at Victoria on route 507 from Waterloo just prior to withdrawal in 1981. *K. Lane*

Below right: The Merlins were replaced by Leyland National 2s on Red Arrow routes. These are proving well able to stand up to the work, and with air suspension, an efficient heating/ventilation system and bright interiors they are proving very popular with passengers. Representing the new breed is brand new LS443 on the circular 500, near Trafalgar Square in 1981. *T. W. Moore*

Above left: London's Daimler Fleetlines are largely confined to the suburbs. DMS1956 is seen at Ealing Broadway on route E1, an Ealing local service on 26 August 1980. *I. P. Cowley*

Left: Although most of the Fleetlines are in suburban areas, DM2529 had penetrated through to Bank while on route 133 in this 1980 view. *I. P. Cowley*

Above: The second generation of rear-engined double-deckers in London comprises MCW Metrobuses and Leyland Titans, both of which are integral vehicles. Representing the former types is M344 at Haven Green. Like the DM/DMS type, the newer vehicles are also largely confined to the suburbs. *I. P. Cowley*

Right: At the time of writing the Titans were all to be found in the north-eastern corner of LT's operating area. T294, one of those built at Workington following the Park Royal collapse, is seen here at Turnpike Lane. *Michael Dryhurst*

Above: Suburban working can be just as arduous as central working in London, as some of the 'suburbs' are towns in their own right. One such place is Kingston-upon-Thames, where LS206, a Leyland National works its way through traffic on route 219 from Weybridge. *I. P. Cowley*

Below: Of all the LT-types the Routemaster can probably be seen on the most diverse of locations. RM2143 is seen at Ealing Broadway while working route 207 on 26 August 1980. This route is shared with DMs as can be seen behind. *I. P. Cowley*

Above: Although the class is now being withdrawn after a short working life, London Transport's BLs (ECW-bodied Bristol LHs) have proved useful on some of the narrow roads on suburban or rural routes especially to the west of London, as they were built to the same dimensions as the RFs they replaced. This BL haunt, the 201 Kingston-Hampton Court via Thames Ditton service disappeared at the end of September 1980. The loading of BL84 would however indicate a demand for the service at certain times of the day. *J. Marsh*

Below: LT's Metro-Scania Metropolitans are confined to garages in south-east London. MD54 is seen at Forest Hill on 12 February 1977. All the MD-class was offered for sale in the summer of 1982. *D. Tate*

Above: At one time Southampton tramcars used to run through the Bargate in the city centre, and had a roof profile not unlike that of the 'Beverley Bar' buses of East Yorkshire. Nowadays only pedestrians have that privilege. Southampton City Transport Leyland Atlantean 250 swings past the Bargate in June 1981. Although a sizeable proportion of SCT buses terminate in the centre, some, such as route 14, carry on to the docks. *Kevin Lane*

Left: Some Southampton local area services are provided by Hants & Dorset. Carrying the local identity 'South Hants', H&D Bristol VRT 389 is seen at Northam on a local Southampton working during June 1982. *Kevin Lane*

Above right: Hants & Dorset dual-purpose Leyland Nationals in the Southampton area are generally used on trunk routes to destinations such as Salisbury. On this occasion, however, 3839, in South Hants livery, was working a local service in the city. *G. K. Gillberry*

Right: One of the more significant trunk routes operated from Southampton by Hants & Dorset is the 47 to Winchester. This was one of the last strongholds of Bristol Lodekkas in the fleet and No 1272 is seen leaving Southampton bus station. Since this photograph, the 47 has become omo, with Bristol VRTs. Wintonline is the local MAP network for Winchester. *I. J. Bovey*

Left: Like many seaside resorts Bournemouth has a requirement for open-top buses in the summer. To increase the availability of such vehicles, many are convertible. Here, Bournemouth Transport's convertible Daimler Fleetline 132 is waiting for customers at Boscombe pier on a June 1981 evening, in open-top guise. *Kevin Lane*

Below left: Bournemouth, like Southampton, is served by its own municipal operator and Hants & Dorset. Bournemouth has a requirement for midibuses on its Centreride service, and employs a variety of motive power thereon, with petrol-engined Bedfords and an electric Dodge. Hants & Dorset's Bristol RE 1638 climbs Commercial Road, Bournemouth passing Bournemouth Transport's Dodge battery midibus in all-over advertising livery for Beales Department store, in June 1982. As Bournemouth Transport is marketed as the Yellow Bus, allover advertising vehicles always display some yellow to the front, hence the yellow front dome. *Kevin Lane*

Right: Like the Southampton/ Bournemouth area, Brighton is served by an NBC subsidiary, Southdown, and its own Borough Transport. In Brighton, an area transport agreement has been in existence since 1938. Brighton Borough Leyland Atlantean No 14 is seen here on Elm Grove, shortly after being painted in the new livery. *Eric Stagg*

Below: Representing the other side of the Brighton Area Transport Service is Southdown No 602, a convertible Bristol VRTSL6G, seen here at Brighton. The BATS agreement also covers Brighton, Hove & District, although in practice BH&D has been absorbed into Southdown. *A. R. J. Frost*

RURAL BUSES

There is still much charm amongst bus operation in the rural districts of Britain. The Victorian railway mania did much to open up rural areas but often, for geographical, political or other reasons, railways did not penetrate the villages and small towns they purported to serve. Thus village stations were often a good way from the actual village; a typical example is Dent, now in Cumbria but then in Yorkshire, where the station is a good number of miles from the village. Thus many of the original rural bus services were those started by railway companies, most notably the Great Western, to act as railway feeders. Since then many of the railways have gone, but the bus services had already established a pattern of bringing people in from remote communities to larger towns, especially those with markets. Now the rural bus services are also diminishing in the same way that the railways have through lack of support from passengers or reductions in local authority subsidies and a changing pattern is emerging. It is in these areas that stage services run by independent operators have sometimes taken over or augmented those provided by the larger operators, often using coaches fitted with power doors and the ability for one-man operation. In places where services have evaporated altogether they have been replaced by community minibuses run by volunteers, and in some other cases by combining the functions of postal collections and deliveries with that of passenger carrying in the form of the postbus. Inevitably this is something of a compromise but it is an intelligent use of resources and very flexible — sometimes the passenger demand is so little that an estate car suffices.

Many of the services into market towns run on market days only; thus for four days a week some small towns may be almost bereft of buses, whilst on market day huge quantities of buses appear as if by magic from miles around.

The nature of rural bus operations is usually vastly different from that in towns. The sophisticated vehicles that are needed to cope with urban traffic

Typifying many of the modern trends in rural bus services this 1973 Bedford YRQ, fitted with Duple 45-seat bodywork, is seen on a schooldays-only Section 30 permit service from Morpeth to Scots Gap. The load is composed solely of scholars with bus passes paid for by the County Council Education Committee. This type of vehicle is often used on stage services by independent operators, being equally suited to schools and contract work, tour and private hire.
C. R. Warn

conditions and loading together with a need to get passengers from A to B as quickly as possible are superfluous in country districts, so smaller, lightweight buses, often with high floors are adequate. The pace of life is different too, and often the driver has his regular clientele and knows that it is more than his life is worth to drive off before Mrs So-and-So has emerged.

Sadly decline has set in badly in rural services and in many instances little more than a skeleton service exists. Some routes are now down to a frequency of only once a month, although once or twice a week is more common. The rise in alternative forms of transport to replace conventional bus services is however indicative of the fact that rural communities, like any others, still need some form of bus service to prevent strangulation. Thus this chapter contains photographs of some less conventional buses as well as the more familiar specimens.

Above: Postbuses, combining the carriage of passengers and of mail, now make a valuable contribution in rural areas where conventional services are uneconomic. Workhorse of the Scottish Postal Board fleet is the 11-seat Commer/Dodge PB2000 with Rootes Maidstone bodywork. This example is seen in rural Lanarkshire. *R. E. Williams*

Below: Certain rural routes, especially in Scotland, render even the use of 11-seat postbus inappropriate. The Tarbert-Skipness post bus service is seen in August 1980 in the charge of a 1979 Avenger estate car. *E. S. Shirras*

Above: The biggest bus ever to operate in Wester Ross is this ex-Hants & Dorset Bristol FLF6L Lodekka in the fleet of Clan Coaches of Kyle. It is seen at Locharron having made a school journey from Plockton over tortuous single track roads.
Stewart J. Brown

Below: An island link. An Alexander-bodied Leyland Leopard of Graham, Paisley, connects with the Cumbrae ferry.
A. J. Douglas

Above: A good many independent operators retain a number of double-deckers for schools and contract work. Such contracts often provide a source of revenue which gives a firm base for stage services. A former Tyne & Wear Atlantean climbs past Fishburn coking plant, on a schools contract for Griersons of Fishburn in September 1981.
Kevin Lane

Below: When the new road between Lambley and Haltswhistle was completed in May 1976 the railway line was closed and replaced by a bus service. Ribble Leyland Leopard PSU4/4R 655 is seen amid wild moorland between Lambley and Alston prior to the changes. Such operating territory is seldom remunerative and is increasingly dependent upon revenue support. *C. R. Warn*

Above: Areas such as the Lake District can obviously use the attraction of local scenery to keep services going, at least during the peak holiday season. In the Lakes, the Mountain Goat network has been established to cater for the needs of visitors and a well-known contributor to these was this Bedford OB, LRO 296. *Peter Thornton*

Below: Also seen in the Lake District is this Ribble Marshall-bodied Leyland Leopard at Grasmere on 26 June 1980. *D. Wayman*

Above: Cumberland Motor Services 608 passes through the restrictive railway arch at Seascale on 14 April 1981. The vehicle, a Plaxton-bodied Leyland Leopard, was formally Trent No 43. *H. S. Postlethwaite*

Below: Although one generally associates ptes with intensive urban service, Greater Manchester Transport's operating area extends some way beyond industrial south-east Lancashire and on to the Pennine escarpment. Former Rochdale Corporation AEC Reliance 24, by then GMT 6024, dating from 1966 is seen leaving Lydgate for Hollingsworth Lake, a popular beauty spot near Littleborough, beyond Rochdale. *I. N. Lynas*

Above: In the depths of rural Cheshire Crosville's SNL403, a Leyland National series B, has just extricated itself from the narrow gap between houses on Oak Road, Mottram St Andrew. Only one journey per day on the E17 is diverted through Mottram St Andrew replacing a withdrawn journey on the E6. *R. Bracegirdle*

Below: On the outskirts of Chester and Saltney circular is being operated by this 1968 Leyland Tiger Cub of Chester City Transport. *D. R. Wootton*

Top: West Yorkshire Leyland National 1006 (DNW 844T) is surrounded by crowns, flags, bunting etc, as Skipton celebrates the Royal Wedding in July 1981. Skipton is an important market town for the Yorkshire Dales. *M. Fowler*

Above: With Whitby and its Abbey evident in the background United Automobile 6041, a dual-purpose Bristol RELL6G, samples the seasonal service to Whitby Laithes during September 1978. *A. Moyes*

Above: Not to be confused with the PTE with the same fleetname, the independent South Yorkshire Road Transport of Pontefract still provides a network of stage services in and around South Yorkshire. Its No 100, a Northern Counties-bodied Fleetline, is seen here speeding through Thorpe Audlin on the Leeds-Doncaster service on 22 August 1980. Few independent operators have the luxury of new double-deckers. *M. Fowler*

Below: The other South Yorkshire has absorbed a good many independents in the Sheffield/Rotherham/Doncaster area and has acquired a fair amount of rural mileage as a result. Renumbered 1087 and repainted in South Yorks livery is this ex-Booth & Fisher AEC Reliance, which was actually new to Maidstone & District. It is seen working service 256 from Harthill to Worksop. *A. R. Kaye*

Above: South Yorkshire PTE No 12 is one of several Series B Leyland National which were diverted from Crosville. It is seen still in Crosville livery with SY logos on either side of the destination box but before the South Yorkshire fleetname was added to the white patches, on a snowy day in 1979 passing Damflask reservoir near High Bradfield. *M. Fowler*

Below: The West and South Yorkshire areas contain a strange mix of urban and rural. Many of the company-operated services in the area link the major towns and in so doing pass through some quite sparsely-populated rural areas and villages. In some ways this is ideal bus-operating territory with large towns acting as attractions for bus passengers for smaller communities. Thus there is quite a high incidence of double-deck working on such routes. Daimler Fleetline 667 of Yorkshire Traction is seen at Clayton West on 24 February 1979, on such a service to Barnsley. *P. L. Stevens*

Above: NBC has had to economise considerably on its widespread rural network in recent years. Where NBC has withdrawn from rural areas, independents have sometimes stepped in to provide services. Trent's Leek-Ashbourne service was taken over by Smiths Tours, Waterhouses, on which is seen its ex-Lancashire United Bristol LH6L with Northern Counties bodywork, UTD 299H. Smiths ceased to trade in 1980 and the business passed to Byrne, Leek. This Bristol was amongst vehicles which went to Byrne after the takeover. *A. Moyes*

Below: Mining is still a major industry in South Yorkshire. A Yorkshire Traction Bristol VRT leaves Kilnhurst, terminus of route 224, en route for Doncaster on Christmas Eve 1980, with typical pithead scenery behind. *M. S. Stokes*

Above: On a Peak District service, Silver Service AEC Reliance WEE 237 still bears its Grimsby-Cleethorpes livery and fleet number as it ascends the steep street of Stanton-in-the-Peak, July 1976, soon after acquisition. *A. Moyes*

Below: Not quite the usual surroundings in which we might expect to find a Derby City Transport bus. Daimler Fleetline/Alexander NAL 53P is seen on a countrified stretch of the trunk 45 route from Derby to Burton-on-Trent. *D. R. Wcotton*

Above: Like the Mountain Goat network in the Lake District the Peak District of Derbyshire has the Peak Park Pathfinder system. This comprises a number of conventional services operated by various operators. The Sunday morning through working from Derby to Ilam in Dovedale, part of the Pathfinder system, then returns to Ashbourne. Trent dual-purpose Leyland Leopard No 136 was working the service on 2 September 1979, when new, and in this view was pulling up from Dovedale to Thorpe. *A. Moyes*

Below: A winter scene in the Peak District, with a Duple-bodied Bedford SB. *D. R. Wootton*

Above: The old name of Enterprise and Silver Dawn has been revived by a Lincoln independent. One of its ex-Monty Moreton Willowbrook-bodied Bedfords is seen here leaving the very rural depot at Waddington on 28 August 1980 with the proprietor at the helm. *M. Fowler*

Below: Sleaford station yard is the terminal point for some of Lincolnshire Road Car Company's services, including what was then in 1979, the 2C and 35. Enjoying the December sunshine is 1053, a Bristol LH6L and 1928, a VRTSL6G, during a layover there. *G. B. Wise*

Above: An ex-Sheffield Burlingham-bodied Leyland Leopard L1 of Stevensons, Uttoxeter, heads for its home town in wintry sunshine. *D. R. Wootton*

Below: GBF 297N, a 1975 Leyland Atlantean of Proctor, Hanley, makes its way home from Leek on a cold winter morning. Such a vehicle is not a typical choice for independent operators although a number in the Stoke area have bought new double-deckers in recent years. *D. R. Wootton*

Left: A Willowbrook dual-purpose-bodied Midland Red Leyland Leopard is seen on service 559, Coventry-Leamington Spa, at Weston under Wetherley on 8 September 1981. Midland Red rural operations have been hit harder than most during the recent decline in bus usage, and this vehicle was carrying a load better suited to a motorcycle and sidecar! *Bob Chisholm*

Centre left: To increase their potential on lightly-loaded rural routes several of the large batch of Midland Red Plaxton-bodied Fords were shortened to midibus proportions. The work was done by the company at its Carlyle works and was made possible by the front-engined layout and relative simplicity of the Ford chassis. The result was nonetheless bizarre! *Chris Howard*

Bottom left: The personal touch is often offered by independents. The driver helps passengers off of FDU 636T, a Ford of Smiths, Tysoe, at Stratford on Avon in January 1980. This is a further instance of a vehicle suited to private hire and excursion work being used on stage service. *G. K. Gillberry*

Above right: One independent formed in recent years is Warstone, Great Wyrley, which has revived the Green Bus Service fleetname once used by Green Bus, Rugeley. The immaculate fleet contains an intriguing mix of vehicles which have made it something of an attraction for enthusiasts. Warstone No 1, an ex-Burnley Pendle Leyland Tiger Cub, is seen at Sandon on 22 September 1982. *R. Selvey*

Below right: Albion Aberdonian/Plaxton Derwent SFW 80 pulls through Park Site, Silverdale on typical mining terrain on a Sunday run in August 1976. This service, operated by Duggins, was taken over by PMT late in 1977. *A. Moyes*

Above left: Over the years services around Haverfordwest have been virtually decimated. The rot set in in the early-1970s when Western Welsh pulled out of the area and bus operation never fully recovered. South Wales Transport took over most of the services and that operator's Leyland Tiger Cub 326 is seen at the Burton Ferry terminus of route 309 on 16 February 1980. Previously operated by Thomas Bros of Port Talbot it has since been withdrawn. In the background is the Cleddau bridge linking Haverfordwest and Milford Haven. *S. K. Miles*

Below left: South Wales AEC Regents had an extended life as they were the only vehicles which could negotiate Plough Corner, Bishopston on the route from Pennard to Swansea. 863 demonstrates the difficulties. These Regents were finally replaced by Bedford YMQS midibuses in 1982. *S. K. Miles*

Above: Much rural bus operation in south-west Wales is in the hands of independent operators. Operated by David Jones of Carmarthen this Duple Dominant-bodied Bedford is seen leaving Llanstephen village for Llanybri. The spelling on the blind is incorrect. *D. M. Stuttard*

Below: One of the furthest points south reached by Crosville is Carmarthen. Aberaeron's Bristol RELL6G paces through Capel Cynon in May 1977, ostensibly working through from Aberystwyth to Carmarthen although in reality it would connect with the Cardigan-Carmarthen service 10 miles further south. However Crosville buses are to be seen in Carmarthen on occasions. Throughout its operating area Crosville runs through delightful countryside; delightful, that is to the observer, if not in terms of potential revenue. *A. Moyes*

Above: Backed by open-cast coal tips, Merthyr Tydfil's Marshall-bodied Dennis Dominator 218 awaits traffic at the Asda supermarket on 21 May 1980. The futuristic styling of the vehicle and scarred landscape create an almost surreal appearance. *A. Moyes*

Below: National Welsh U1769, a 1969 Leyland Leopard, makes its way through Barry Docks prior to the implementation of MAP route revisions under the Barrivale title. *A. Moyes*

Above: South Wales Leyland National 774 on a working from Glyncorrwg climbs through Cymer en route to Port Talbot and Sandfields Estate on 30 March 1981. *S. K. Miles*

Below: This Bristol RELL6L then operated by Jones Omnibus Co of Aberbeeg, tackles the switchback of Cwmtillery in July 1980. The vehicle carried NBC blue livery. Jones has since been absorbed into National Welsh and lost its distinctive blue in favour of poppy red. *A. Moyes*

Above: Like several other operators National Welsh has used smaller vehicles for certain rural routes. A Village Bus network is operated by green and yellow-liveried Leyland 440EAs with Asco bodywork and two of these, MD1177 and MD1377 are seen at Cowbridge town hall in 1980. *A. Moyes*

Below: The large and the small of South Wales Transport, seen here at Oystermouth bus station. On the left is a Reebur-bodied Bedford CF No 96, about to work an Oystermouth-Bishopston Gower Pony journey while 990, on a Morriston Hospital-Caswell Bay working, is a standard NBC Bristol VRT. *S. K. Miles*

Above: An earlier vehicle on Gower Pony operations of South Wales was this Dormobile-bodied Ford Transit. As can be seen stretches of the route are limited in passenger potential, with little habitation. However, the quadruped ponies of the Gower peninsula seem to be taking some interest in their vehicular namesake. *NBC*

Below: Some independent operators also make use of minibuses and Bryn Melyn Motor Services' Ford Transit SLG 177R is seen three miles from World's End on the Llangollen-Pentredwr service. *M. Fowler*

Top: A Bedford VAS of Harding's Coaches travels through a typical Somerset lane near Wiveliscombe. *Viewfinder*

Above: Shaftesbury, Dorset, is border territory between Hants & Dorset and Western National. A former coach Bristol MW of Hants & Dorset is seen here on the A30 bound for Shaftesbury in October 1974. *R. Brown*

Above: During the mid-1970s Western National took delivery of several Plaxton coach-bodied Bristol LHs. These sometimes appeared on long-distance routes, even working through to London on some occasions (one wonders what the original Elliotts would have thought of such a vehicle on Royal Blue services!) They are ideally suited to some of the rural routes around Somerset and Dorset, and here WNOC 3102 is seen on a country route at Dorchester.
Michael Dryhurst

Below: An usual type of vehicle in the Hants & Dorset fleet was the ECW-bodied Ford R1014. These vehicles came at a time when NBC was taking more lightweight buses than usual, and their appearance could easily convince the unwary that they were Bristols. *Michael Dryhurst*

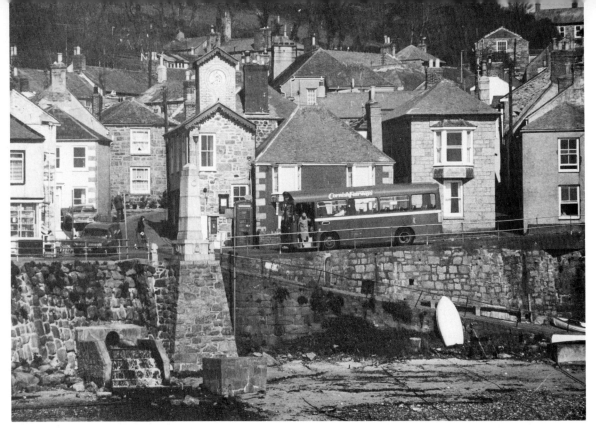

Above: Well camouflaged, Western National 1557, a Bristol LH6L sets down on the quay at Mousehole, Cornwall. It has just arrived from Penzance in April 1981. Such services are obviously seasonal in demand and lead to certain operational problems. The LHS is an ideal vehicle for operation is such confined spaces. *A. Moyes*

Below: Mousehole's local operator, Harvey, also finds the Bristol LHS a useful tool for its stage work. This LHS6L has Marshall bodywork and was seen above Newlyn making for home. *A. Moyes*

Above: AEC Regents featured in many NBC fleets, but none is now used on public service. This Devon General Regent V is seen passing Cockwood Harbour on a Sunday morning working from Exeter to Dawlish Warren. *A. R. Kaye*

Below: Drummer Street bus station Cambridge in December 1980. On the left is an Eastern Counties Willowbrook-bodied Leopard with LH920, an ECW-bodied Bristol LH nearer the camera. *Kevin Lane*

Left: An Eastern National Bedford YMQS midibus with Wadham Stringer Vanguard bodywork is seen departing Dedham for Colchester on 8 July 1981. Although mainly for rural work these vehicles feature coach seats and often work the longer-distance Highwayman express services. At the time of writing these vehicles were unique in NBC service, although two subsidiaries have Lex-bodied YMQSs. *G. R. Mortimer*

Right: Prior to the closure of the service in 1981 this 11-seat Commer post bus was seen in Dedham on an East Bergholt-Colchester working on 12 May 1980. This particular vehicle inaugurated the service in 1975 and remained on it until replaced just before the service was withdrawn. *G. R. Mortimer*

Right: Sibley, Halstead, operates this attractive Plaxton-bodied Bedford CF on a Halstead shopping service. The Mini Supreme is a good compromise between a full-size coach and a minibus.
G. R. Mills

Left: In attractive East Anglian countryside is an Eastern Counties Alexander/Ford integral midibus carrying that unhelpful destination 'Service'.

Right: Community buses are increasing as an alternative form of rural transport. This Ford Transit was used on the Norfolk community bus service and was operated by Eastern Counties. It is seen at Bale.

Above: JDW, Ipswich, went out of business during 1981 at a time when many long-established independents were disappearing. An unusual vehicle to find on a local service is PDX 171W, a Bedford YMT with Van Hool bodywork, leaving the Old Cattle Market, Ipswich on 6 February 1981 amid a cloud of exhaust fumes. Normally one would expect to find Van Hool Alizée-bodied coaches on extended tour or long-distance express work. *I. P. Cowley*

Below: Much of the Suffolk countryside is unspoiled, and there is still a strong tradition of independent bus operation. Beestons (Hadleigh) Ltd, operates a Hadleigh-Ipswich service and in February 1973 it too used an unlikely vehicle on the service, a Caetano Cascais II-bodied Bedford. *G. R. Mortimer*

Above: There is often a surprising amount of co-operation between independents and NBC operators in rural areas. This Duple-bodied Bedford of Beestons was seen on hire to Eastern Counties in this view. *R. A. Flower*

Below: The Duple Dominant bus body is a popular choice amongst independents for rural work and this Duple Dominant-bodied Bedford YMT of H. C. Chambers was seen leaving Colchester on a Bury St Edmunds service on 13 March 1981. *I. P. Cowley*

Top: United Counties was one NBC operator to use
lightweights to a large extent. Two of its
Willowbrook-bodied Bedfords are seen here in Hitchin.
Kevin Lane

Above: More usual NBC fare is this United Counties Leyland
National 557, seen near Whipsnade Zoo. *Kevin Lane*

Above: Diminishing loads on services in rural areas and small towns have led NBC to aim for a different approach in some cases. Although current policy does not favour lightweights the smaller Bedfords, which use the same componentry as their larger brethren have found places in some fleets. United Counties uses these attractive Lex-bodied Bedford YMQSs on Leighton Buzzard services. *Kevin Lane*

Below: A larger United Counties bus is 283, a Bristol RELH6G with dual purpose bodywork, seen here loading in Aylesbury. *Kevin Lane*

Left: During the late-1970s NBC tried its own conversions of full-size Fords to midibuses. As mentioned earlier many were done by Midland Red. Alder Valley also had a go and 798 (TRD 724N), seen at Marlow on 27 April 1980, was a conversion of an ECW-bodied Ford. The result was not terribly elegant! *G. K. Gillberry*

Left: Deep in rural Kent, East Kent Leyland National 1349 picks up at Coldred on the Dover-Eythorne service. *A. Moyes*

Right: London Country has also tried different approaches to rural bus operation including Sunday service for walkers and the like in the Sevenoaks and Dorking areas. One of that company's Bristol LHSs is seen at Bitchet Common on a Rambler's Bus service.

Left: An attempt was made to attract more custom in the picturesque Eden Valley in Kent. Proclaiming itself proudly as the Eden Valley Village Bus is this Plaxton-bodied Ford of Maidstone & District.

Right: A similar service was introduced in conjunction with Hertfordshire County Council in the Lea Valley. Obviously LCBS was rather unsure of the correct spelling and the destination blind spelt it one way whilst bets were hedged by the use of slip boards spelling its another! Publicity material was equally ambiguous. Leyland National SNB163 is seen at Hayes Hill in the summer of 1981, after a route revision allowing larger vehicles than previously. *S. J. Butler*

Above: Snow does fall in Surrey sometimes as shown by this view of London Country Leyland Atlantean AN123 at Lee Street, Horley. *D. Trevor Rowe*

Below: The Guildford area is served by two NBC subsidiaries and several independents. Some of the most rural routes in the area are run by Tillingbourne Bus of Gomshall. MPE 248P is one of Tillingbourne's Plaxton-bodied Bedfords, seen nearing Busbridge Lakes on a Sunday morning working of the 'Scenic Circular'. *P. R. Nuttal*

Above: A Southdown dual-door Bristol threads its way past Rottingdean pond in a classically English setting. No doubt philosophers could while away many a happy hour debating the enigmatic message carried on the advertisement!
A. R. J. Frost

Below: A 1959 AEC Reliance, formerly of Reading Corporation, is seen passing through the ford at Tarrant Monkton, Dorset, on 24 December 1980, whilst in service with the Stanbridge and Crichel Bus Co Ltd. *G. K. Gillberry*

COACHING & CONTRACTS

Coaching is largely involved with the leisure side of the bus industry, covering as it does express work, excursions and tours. Coaching had its heyday in the 1930s when coach companies vied with each other for the ultimate in luxury. Indeed, certain operators made quite a name for themselves in the field of luxury; Royal Blue of course was famed for its standards of comfort and service. In those days coaching was slow; vehicles were severely restricted in speed, despite the comparatively light traffic, because the roads were not good enough. Coach travel was not particularly cheap, but then neither was rail travel so coaches carved quite a niche for themselves.

As railways began to pick up after the war, so coaches fell behind, but the opening of Britain's first major motorway, the M1, in 1959 led to a great upturn in the coach's fortunes. As soon as the motorway opened, two major operators had new vehicles ready and waiting; Midland Red had its own BMMO CM5 coach whilst Ribble subsidiary Standerwick had its highly luxurious Gay Hostess coaches — double-deckers with all mod cons, including the kitchen sink, toilet and, as its name implied, a hostess. (In those days, the literal meaning of the word 'gay' was still applicable.) Both these vehicles were capable of speeds up to three times the previous legal maximum, and express coaching was set to enter a new era.

Nowadays, the motorway network covers the largest part of the country and deregulation in 1980 led to fare reductions, so the express coach is a more viable proposition. Journey times are still usually longer than those for rail, but the difference is not as marked even given the 70mph limit which the two pioneers were well able to exceed, and fares are in a different league.

By 1970 the larger operators had been nationalised and the National Express division of National Bus Company has a very wide network of express services, comprising high frequency, high-speed services to most major centres and a less frequent but tighter web of cross-country routes. In certain instances these almost provide a rural stage service.

The pattern of excursions and tours has gone through a less dramatic metamorphosis over the years and the traditional day, halfday or evening excursion is still fairly popular. Twenty years ago, however, the Continental tour would have been most prestigious but today with the ready availability of suitable coaches and a much improved road network the extended tour to the continent is much more commonplace and is one of the more lucrative markets for a wide range of operators.

Local sightseeing tours, running on a regular headway basis are also quite widespread. Usually these are operated by buses rather than coaches and double-deckers are often favoured with their obvious benefit of a high vantage point. Quite a number of operators now offer Round London Sightseeing tours and even that run by London Transport is often subcontracted, most notably to Obsolete Fleet which can now even provide forward-entrance Routemasters for the tour.

Contract work is a very valuable part of bus operation, and is often the most important part of an operator's income. Contracts often take the form of a works' service, sometimes provided free of charge by employers, though more often the employees contribute towards the cost. The other important source of contract work is in taking children to school from outlaying areas.

National Express claims over 3,000 destinations, more than any other surface carrier in the UK. Since deregulation concentration has been on high-speed trunk motorway services, such as that shown here between London and Newcastle. Heavy rain makes the going tough on the M1 in Nottinghamshire for this Plaxton-bodied Leyland Leopard.
T. W. Moore

Above: The Scottish Bus Group has a somewhat individualistic line in coaches. Quite a rarity in southern Britain is this Alexander T-type-bodied Seddon Pennine VII, Western SMT CS2950, seen leaving Dunstable for Glasgow on the service worked jointing with Premier Travel on Fridays and Sundays in the summer. *Kevin Lane*

Below: The Scottish Bus Group's well-known Alexander M-type motorway coaches are being phased out in favour of new Duple-bodied vehicles. Western SMT Volvo B10M KV115 moves into position on a damp evening at Victoria prior to working the night service to Glasgow. *Michael Dryhurst*

Above: The M8 between Glasgow and Edinburgh has opened up a good opportunity for a high-speed coach link between Scotland's two principal cities. Eastern Scottish Seddon Pennine VII, ZS869A, awaits departure for Edinburgh. *David Stuttard*

Below: Prior to deregulation only a small handful of independent operators worked daily long-distance express services. Perhaps the most important was Yelloway, Rochdale, which had the monopoly on services from the north-west to Cheltenham and points west. An extension of that basic service was the South-West Clipper from Yorkshire and two Yelloway AEC Reliances are seen loading up in Sheffield for that service. *Alan Hilton*

Left: Yorkshire has several important centres of population which have always warranted good bus services and in recent years an express network has built up, centred mainly on Sheffield. Yorkshire Traction's 154 a Plaxton-bodied Leyland Leopard, stands at Penistone Church while on service X68 from Halifax to Huddersfield to Sheffield. *Alan Hilton*

Right: On hire to National Travel one of East Yorkshire's Leyland Leopard PSU3C/4s with Plaxton Supreme bodywork enters the Bull Ring centre, Birmingham on a service to Cheltenham. *T. W. Moore*

Left: The main industrial area of northern England cuts a band across from Liverpool via Manchester to West and South Yorkshire. However in the middle of this highly-populated belt is one of the wildest stretches of countryside in England. Two Crosville Bristol RELHs head across the Pennines on a summer-only service from Stockport and Oldham to Filey. *D. Wayman*

Left: Another Trans-Pennine route is that from Manchester to Nottingham, which is now a basic corridor for routes between the north-west and the East Midlands/East Anglia. One of six Leyland Leopards with Alexander T-type bodywork, Trent 114 leaves Buxton Market Place on the 952 Manchester-Nottingham express. *A. Moyes*

Right: A Midland Red Leyland Leopard in National Express livery, HHA 198L speeds along the M4 in what would appear to be a posed shot.

Above: A later Leyland Leopard of Midland Red, JOX 447P passes through Kenilworth on a Cardiff-Birmingham journey. *T. W. Moore*

Below: Cheltenham is of course a major destination with its important connectional facilities. National Travel (South West) Plaxton-bodied Leopard 267 is seen on the Ipswich-Cheltenham Eastlander turning in the square at Dunstable. *Kevin Lane*

Above: A touch of glamour is provided on the joint Trathens-National London-Plymouth Rapide service, which uses Neoplan Skyliner six-wheel double-deckers. As UK construction and use regulations demand an emergency exit the rear face has been modified somewhat, giving a rather dated appearance. *B. Grigg*

Below: The joint South Wales Transport/Bristol Omnibus Expresswest service between Haverfordwest and Bristol provides a mix of interurban motorway running and rural stage work. On the interurban section, South Wales 169, a Duple-bodied Leyland Leopard calls at Cardiff. A Cardiff City Transport Bristol VRT/Alexander overtakes. *S. Morris*

Above: Eastern National's Highwayman network in eastern England is run as a cross between excursion and express. Bedford YMT 1214 works the 806 Highwayman and was photographed in Dunstable on its Milton Keynes-Harwich journey in April 1981. *Kevin Lane*

Below: Like Yelloway, Premier is an old-established express operator. An Alexander-bodied AEC Reliance, VER 262L, is seen on a Cambridge-Oxford service, jointly run by Percival of Oxford & Cambridge and Premier Travel, in Dunstable in August 1980. Surprisingly the coach was then in service with Percivals and not Premier, hence the lack of destination equipment. *Kevin Lane*

Above: A Plaxton-bodied Leyland Leopard, operated by Grey-Green, is seen on 14 July 1972 on service X17 from Harwich to Scotland at Bradfield amid attractive Suffolk countryside. *G. R. Mortimer*

Below: East Kent 8027, a 1973 AEC Reliance is seen unloading on the front at Margate on Easter Monday 1981, before returning to London. *Kevin Lane*

Above: Victoria coach station is a main centre of operations for National Express services. In this view it was at its busiest, on a Friday in late-July. Although many of the coaches are in allover white, variety is provided by the Southdown Leopard in traditional livery (far left), a Premier Travel AEC Reliance in the foreground, a Grey-Green Leopard passing in front of the Southdown coach and a Bristol VRT double-deck coach of Alder Valley on a Londonlink service.
C. Nash

Below: One of the first responses to deregulation was the formation of British Coachways, a consortium of independent operators which intended to take on National Express as a competitor. In the event the organisation was to crumble quickly and is now but a shadow of its former self. However it was largely responsible for the new era of cheap travel. A Grey-Green Leyland Leopard and a Volvo of Morris Bros, Swansea, the latter in full BC livery, arrive at Kings Cross.
Malcolm Keeley

Top: Southdown 1329, a Plaxton–bodied Leyland Leopard, speeds along the Brighton Road on the 064 service from Eastbourne and Brighton to London. *Michael Dryhurst*

Above: Formerly Southdown 1805, this 1970 Duple-bodied Leyland Leopard later passed to Hants & Dorset as No 3074. It is seen swinging out of Bournemouth coach station in June 1981. *Kevin Lane*

Above: This Roe-bodied Leyland Atlantean JWF 47W, was bought for use on Limebourne Coaches' Cityrama tours of London. *Kevin Lane*

Below: Employed on the London Transport Round London Sightseeing Tour is this ex-Samuelsons 1970 Leyland Leopard, AYU 469H, in LT red livery. *G. R. Mills*

Above: A number of interesting vehicles find their way on to the sightseeing tour. In August 1978 it was the turn of this ex-Northern General forward-entrance Routemaster. *D. M. Stuttard*

Below: Obsolete Fleet acquired several ex-Midland Red D9s for the Round London Sightseeing Tour, most of which were converted to open top. In this view OM2 is seen in Oxford Street on a Christmas lights service. *L. D. S. Dolan*

Above: West Yorkshire's York city tours have always been a popular attraction. During the summer of 1980 a Leyland Leopard is seen on the tour with the Minster in the background. *D. Akrigg*

Below: An Alexander (Midland) Duple-bodied Leyland Leopard pulls out of Buchanan Street bus station on a Glasgow city tour. *T. E. Sutch*

Above: In addition to its Express division National Travel has an active Holidays division. Midland Red 614, a Plaxton-bodied Leyland Leopard is seen in Edinburgh on a Scottish extended tour. *G. Coxon*

Below: This Plaxton-bodied Ford of Shearings/Ribblesdale had found itself a good way from home when photographed outside the John O' Groats Hotel during a northern Highlands and Speyside tour in August 1981. *G. B. Wise*

Left: Not surprisingly East Kent performs various contracts for Dover docks. Suitably bedecked for the Seaspeed Hovercraft service, 1841, an Alexander-bodied Daimler Fleetline having arrived in 1978 from Potteries, shuttles between East Dock and Marine station. *A. Moyes*

Left: Towards the end of their working lives, in July 1981, a collection of East Kent AEC Regents worked a contract service to provide transport for the British Open Golf Championship at Sandwich. *C. W. Routh*

Right: An Alder Valley Bristol VRT, painted in allover advertising livery for Dataskil proves a useful giraffe-feeding platform. The bus was hired by Dataskil to provide trips to Windsor Safari Park for 'educational priority' school children in Reading to celebrate its 10th anniversary. *Dataskil*

Left: An unusual vehicle used by Jones, Flint, on school work is this ex-North Western Strachans-bodied Bedford VAL, AJA 139B. The vehicle, which was originally built for the Altrincham-Warrington service via the notorious Dunham Massey canal overbridge, is now painted somewhat garishly to advertise Jones' British Leyland car dealership. *A. Moyes*

Right: A somewhat bizarre load, comprising Snow White plus attendant dwarfs joins a National Express Leyland Leopard at Victoria.

BACK-UP

The processes involved in keeping buses on the road are complex. It is not really possible to portray in pictures the traffic function, although all the foregoing pictures in their own way give testimony to the work of traffic departments. However, publicity and marketing are really functions of the traffic department in the broader sense and some photographs of vehicles used in that way are included in this section.

The engineering department carries the responsibility for ensuring that sufficient vehicles are available for service at any one time and as vehicles get more complicated and legislation more demanding the need for extensive maintenance facilities is increased.

Day to day maintenance, which includes refuelling, cleaning etc, is the responsibility of local depots or garages. These range in size from substantial buildings in large towns housing up to 200 vehicles, down to rural outstations which are little more than sheds for a couple of vehicles. The last are less common than they were; it is no longer economical for large companies to retain numbers of small depots scattered throughout their operating area, and the trend now is towards larger allocations to a smaller number of garages.

Larger bus garages, nowadays, often have more in the way of engineering facilities, and most medium-sized and smaller fleets' garages are able to cover the whole range of maintenance. The largest operators have centralised engineering works; London Transport has its overhaul works at Aldenham, for example, where the actual overhaul of all LT vehicles is undertaken. It also has facilities at Chiswick where major components are overhauled or reconditioned and supplied to Aldenham.

A large garage employs a substantial number of people in addition to platform staff and can be kept working 24hr per day, with first departures in the morning at around 04.00hrs and last vehicles running in after 24.00hrs. In the intervening fours hours maintenance work, cleaning work, cleaning and such like may continue.

A line up of London Transport Leyland Nationals and a Routemaster prepare to leave Norbiton garage to work outer London suburban routes. *J. Rickard*

Left: The former Midland Red depot in Stourbridge, now owned by West Midlands PTE is also used as a terminal point for services. Daimler Fleetline 6203, an ex-Midland Red vehicle, awaits departure on an evening run to Wednesbury. *P. R. Nuttall*

Below left: Many rural garages and outstations are little more than large sheds. Typical is that of East Kent at Deal, with a Leyland National and a Ford outside. *Eric Baldock*

Right: Receiving attention over the pits at Greater Manchester Transport's Bury garage is this Bristol RESL6G with Marshall bodywork No 300, which was new to North Western. *A. Moyes*

Below: Call for buses in Plymouth on a bank holiday is obviously limited judging by this line up of Leyland Atlanteans at Plymouth City depot on August Bank Holiday 1972. *L. M. Punnett*

Left: Northern General 4647, a Leyland National takes a shower at Stanley garage. *G. Coxon*

Below: The rear ends of rear-engined double-deckers are not easy to clean mechanically due to their awkward shape. South Yorkshire PTE has a solution, as shown by Atlantean 1614.

Right: At smaller garages a simpler, open-air gantry washer is usually adequate. Having fuelled and watered South Wales Leopard 169 is washed at Haverfordwest depot in October 1981 prior to leaving for Bristol on an Expresswest working. *S. K. Miles*

Below right: Fulwell garage of London Transport has recently been re-equipped with a Britannia Streamline washer. M47, a Metrobus, is cleaned in this drive-through washer before working the 285.

Far left: A Derby City Transport Daimler CVG6 with Roe bodywork is separated from its chassis for major overhaul work. *T. W. Moore*

Left: A West Midland PTE Daimler Fleetline is lifted up on jacks during overhaul work.

Below left: A well-equipped and attractive maintenance area is now a feature of Merseyside PTE's Prince Alfred Road garage.

Right: London Transport has very extensive overhaul facilities. The final stage overhaul work is repainting, and an unidentified Routemaster is here being spray painted. To assist their task the painters are raised and lowered on elevating catwalks either side of the bus.

Below: Few independent operators can afford workshops like those of major undertakings. Most are able to provide adequate facilities, however, and this simple ramp arrangement allows a good many tasks to be carried out by The Eden, West Auckland, Co Durham. Plaxton-bodied Leyland Leopard UUP 660K receives steam cleaning. *G. Coxon*

Left: Not surprisingly quite a high proportion of towing vehicles begin life as buses or coaches. This one of Midland Red shows obvious origins as a Plaxton Panorama-bodied Leyland Leopard.
R. Heathcote

Left: This former Eastern Scottish Bristol Lodekka has also been reduced to towing wagon status. *A. J. Douglas*

Below: Underfloor-engine coaches often make rather stylish breakdown tenders. This Crosville recovery vehicle at Chester was formerly a Bristol MW.
Adrian Pearson

Right: Alder Valley has a purpose–built ERF breakdown lorry. On 18 July 1981 it had a lengthy run up to London to recover a Leyland National which had failed on the X12 at Victoria. As Leyland National buses are not standard fare on the X12 it is possible that that too had been replacing a failed vehicle. *C. Nash*

Right: Amongst the finer towing vehicles is that used by Hyndburn. It is a 1949 Guy Arab III saloon. *John Robinson*

Below: This Burlingham Seagull-bodied Bedford looked rather the worse for wear when seen at White House Service Station, Nettlebed, Oxon, in March 1973. *T. H. J. Dethridge*

Above: London Country Leyland National LN7 has become a familiar sight in its new role as travelling sales bus.
D. M. Stuttard

Below: 1981 was the International Year of Disabled People and several ex-City of Oxford Fleetlines were converted into disabled people's information buses. They toured the country and KFC 377G was photographed in Luton. *Kevin Lane*

Above: London Country AEC Swift SM488 was used to publicise Weyfarer services after MAP revisions in the Guildford and Woking area. *K. Pratt*

Below: This West Midlands (ex-Birmingham) Daimler CVG6 enjoyed an extended life as a sales bus for WMPTE travel cards, for which it received a bright, if a little undignified colour scheme. It is seen here in Brownhills. *Adrian Pearson*

Above: Still in pre-NBC green, London Country RT981 sets out on a training run from St Albans garage in March 1980. *Kevin Lane*

Below: Cleveland Transit trainer H12, a 1964 Park Royal-bodied Atlantean is seen in Darlington. A United Automobile Plaxton-bodied Bristol RE coach passes on the London service. *Kevin Lane*